Butternut & Blue
Threads of the Civil War

By Barbara Brackman & Karla Menaugh

Contents

"A great many Rebel prisoners of war are quartered [near Columbus, Ohio]. They were a motley set, dressed in garments of every conceivable style, material and color, yellow, red, blue, gray, butternut, etc. Around some, dirty old bed quilts were thrown, pieces of carpeting, ragged blankets, etc."

— Letter from Nancy Dunlevy Anderson, March 17, 1862. *Life and Letters of Judge Thomas J. Anderson and Wife,* edited by James H. Anderson (J. Heer, 1904) Pg. 198

SUNFLOWER PATTERN CO-OPERATIVE

First edition, second printing
ISBN: 0-9725457-1-9

Printed in the United States of America by Boelte-Hall Litho, Inc., Roeland Park, Kansas

Threads of the Civil War

Butternut, or white walnut, woodcut by Barbara Brackman, 2003

History notes by Barbara Brackman, author of *Quilts from the Civil War* and *Civil War Women*

Butternut

The Civil War lingers in American memory in shades of Union blue and Confederate gray. But gray was the formal color, the uniform of pomp and circumstance, of Lee and Jackson and the plantation aristocracy. The realities of everyday life, especially in the South, demanded a make-do wardrobe.

With very few factories to supply uniforms or even yard goods, the Southern soldier relied on the Southern woman's ingenuity.

Tryphena Fox wrote her mother in 1864 about a trade her physician husband negotiated with a patient in Mississippi. "She made him a beautiful piece of gray homespun jeans. It is as fine & pretty as boughten goods & makes him a nice warm coat & pr. of pants. I made the pants & trimmed them with a side strip of black velvet & he hired the coat made – I am very proud of the suit for him – Now he looks quite genteel as well as Confederate." [1]

The gray jeans fabric Tryphena used was probably wool and, like our blue jeans today, woven of contrasting dark and light yarns. The dye was probably indigo, which produces a variety of blues. Rather than a solid neutral gray, the Confederate gray appears to our eyes as a light blue, a blue flecked with white. Englishman Henry Yates Thompson described a group of Confederates he met on a river boat as "hirsute soldiers in light blue great coats and capes." [2] Winslow Homer's painting, *Prisoners From the Front*, shows three Southerners in steel blue clothing with brass buttons, their gray garb lighter in shade but similar in hue to that of their Union captor.

Tryphena's homespun gray was a luxury to many Southerners, like those Thompson observed at a Nashville prison. "Only one of the prisoners had a uniform, an artillery man in a buff [tan] jacket with red facings. The mass of the rebels in the west fight in their common clothes."[3] With little access to imported dyes and the manufactured cloth of Europe or New England, the rural Southern army relied on an unofficial uniform of butternut. Home-dyed with the hulls and bark of the White Walnut tree (Juglans cinerea), butternut cloth is a golden brown. Walnut dyes were simple to produce, requiring only a thicket of America's common tree. Two bushels of bark colored twenty yards of cloth when heated and steeped. The dyer could add copperas (ferrous sulphate), which probably produced a faster color and a different shade, but a pleasant variety of medium browns could be obtained with the nut or bark alone.

With very few factories to supply uniforms or even yard goods, the Southern soldier relied on the Southern woman's ingenuity. Henry Thompson noted that a good many of the rebel prisoners, "some fifty or sixty men [wore] various shades of butternut." [4] Butternut or "brown jeans" or "copperas" clothing was so common that the term "butternut" became a synonym for "rebel." Benjamin F. McIntyre was a Union soldier in Springfield, Missouri. "Our company was formed into a line this morning – and informed it would be our duty to guard butternut prisoners," a duty he resented, considering it "menial service – acting as guard over the few miserable bushwhackers who are confined here." [5]

The most famous bushwhacker or irregular Confederate guerrilla fighter was William Quantrill, who burned the anti-slavery town of Lawrence, Kansas, in 1863, killing nearly 200 men and boys. Many of Quantrill's raiders wore butternut. Forty years later, a Lawrence newspaper took note of an old man from Missouri who came to town "wearing a butternut suit like the border ruffians wore during the war. All of Quantrell's (sic) men had on these suits during the raid and six months after that time if a man had appeared in town wearing such a suit he would have been shot – The old settlers at once noticed his uniform and recalled the hated clothes of the men who dealt death wherever they struck." [6]

Carte de visite, 1868, Galena, Illinois, unknown man in a wool suit, similar to what gray home-spun looked like.

Throughout North and South the dye symbolized Confederate loyalties. In Indiana during the War, William Merks Rock recalled the Knights of the Golden Circle, a semi-secret society of Northerners with Southern sympathies. "I saw many butternut pins, the emblem worn by disloyal women."[7]

Butternut dyes all natural fibers – wool, cotton, and linen, as well as silk (butternut-dyed silk seems an odd combination of country and city.) Butternut home-spun uniforms were undoubtedly wool rather than cotton, but cotton-wool combinations, called linsey, jeans, hickory cloth, or Kentucky cloth, were also popular. In combination cloth, the cotton was often left white and the wool dyed, which would produced a lighter-appearing fabric, a medium brown flecked with white.

What color was butternut? We can still see the shade of brown jeans fabric in the uniform of the carpenter, the bricklayer, the farmer and the cowboy. Although dyed with synthetic rather than natural dye, today's Carharrt work clothing is similar to the traditional light brown butternut of the nineteenth century. Carharrt pants, coveralls and jackets are made of a sturdy cotton duck, probably dyed in the cloth stage, rather than in the yarn stage like nineteenth-century jeans, which were often woven of different colored warp and weft. New Carharrts are a plain yellow brown that fades lighter and duller over time.

Nineteenth-century writers described walnut-dyed cloth with some variability. Albert D. Richardson noted Rebel Butternuts dressed in "cinnamon-hued home-spun." [8] Henry Thompson nearly stepped on a dead Confederate in the woods. "[It] gave me a shock – his butternut clothing being the same colour as the leaves he was lying on."[9] Elijah Bemiss in an 1815 dye manual noted that butternut yielded various shades of brown depending on the heat of the dye bath and the proportion and order of walnut and copperas. "Sometimes more of one sort, and sometimes less – Thus I leave it to the discretion of the dyer, to vary them as he or she pleases – " [10]

MORE ➤

In choosing butternut-shaded cottons today, quiltmakers and re-enactors should look for golden browns in a variety of values from light to dark. Yellow browns with a touch of green are good. Avoid reddish browns (despite Richardson's "cinnamon-hued" description), which in the nineteenth century were dyed with commercial dyes such as madder rather than home-dyed walnut. Also avoid very deep browns, since descriptions of butternut and copperas consistently indicate medium to light browns.

Blue

The Union uniform was far more consistent than Confederate garb. The North had factories for cloth and clothing production, access to wool and to the imported indigo and Prussian blue dyes to color it. These dyes were the two most common blue coloring agents for natural fibers at the time, and both produce the dark blue wool typical of the Union Army. Indigo, a vegetable dye derived from the roots of the indigo plant, was more expensive. Prussian blue, a mineral dye, was given its name because of its popularity in dyeing military uniforms.

Blue coats identified the hated Federals throughout the South. Even after the War, the shade evoked emotions. In South Carolina in 1866, Ella Clanton Thomas's daughter Mary Bell pointed out a hitchhiker. "'Oh Ma there is a Yankee.' I looked and saw a young strong man – .'Why have you the slightest idea that I would take you in the Carriage to ride with me – and you a Yankee. He hastened to say he was not. 'Well,' I said, 'let me give you a little advice. If you wish much kindness shown to you don't travel through this portion of the country wearing blue pants.'" [11]

Quiltmakers and re-enactors looking for Yankee blue should find what we call navy, a dark neutral blue with no purple or greenish tints. This blackish blue, the color of the field in the Union flag, symbolizes the Union uniform.

Indigo, woodcut by Barbara Brackman, 2003

Reproduction Quilts

Butternuts doing dastardly deeds, torturing babies and shooting dogs (detail) by Thomas Nast in *Harper's Weekly*

We've seen quilts of butternut and blue, possibly stitched of scraps left over from the War years. It's important to remember that the Southern homespun fabrics were wools or combination wool/cotton plains, plaids and checks. In the quilts in this book, our interpretations of a variety of mid-nineteenth-century quilts, we used much artistic license.

First of all, we use printed cottons – the old home-dyed fabrics were never printed. We love prints, but a two-colored quilt of plain butternut and blue would be dramatic. We didn't narrow our color range to the authentic shades of butternut and blue. We used a variety of browns, some with reddish tones, and we added very dark and very light browns for contrast. Our blues included light blues, the bright blues that were popular in the 1850s and 1860s for women's clothing dyed with Prussian blue, and the pale gray indigo blues known as Cadet blue, most popular after 1890. We added other colors to the palette for visual impact and we're giving you the same artistic license to interpret the antique quilt designs in the fabrics and shades that appeal to you.

The **Butternut and Blue** fabric collection that Barbara Brackman and Terry Clothier Thompson designed for Moda is colored with the modern quiltmakers' taste in mind. The Yankee Blue colorway is a little lighter and brighter than the true Union navy blue and the Butternut Gold colorway is much more subdued than much of the naturally dyed butternuts of the nineteenth century. We added the Rebel Red and Hickory Brown colorways for contrast and impact. We suggest you collect a fabric palette with a wide variety of blues, golds, browns, tans and reds.

1. Letter from Tryphena Blanche Fox, October 14, 1864. *A Northern Woman in the Plantation South,* edited by Wilma King (University of South Carolina Press, 1993) Pg. 141.

2. Diary entry by Henry Yates Thompson, November 21, 1863. *An Englishman in America's Civil War,* edited by Sir Christopher Chancellor (London: Sidgwick and Jackson, 1971) Pg. 144.

3. Thompson, November 17, 1863. Pg. 136.

4. Thompson, ibid.

5. *Federals on the Frontier:* The Diary of Benjamin F. McIntyre, edited by Nannie M. Tilley (Austin: University of Texas Press, 1963)

6. *Lawrence Daily World,* February 24, 1903, Pg. 3.

7. William Merks Rock, *Pioneer Days in Indiana and Kansas* (Lyndon, Kansas: By the Author, 1929).

8. A.D.Richardson, *The Secret Service, the Field, the Dungeon, and the Escape.* (Hartford: American Publishing Co, 1865) Pg. 256.

9. Thompson, November 27, 1863. Pg. 166.

10. Elijah Bemiss *The Dyer's Companion* (New York: Evert Duyckinck, 1815) Reprint, 1973, Dover Publications. Pg. 33.

11. Diary entry by Ella Clanton Thomas, September 20, 1866. The Secret Eye: *The Journal of Ella Gertrude Clanton Thomas,* edited by Virginia Ingraham Burr (Chapel Hill: University of North Carolina Press, 1990)

Midnight Garden

The inspiration for this appliqué was a mid-nineteenth century wool appliqué, a basket of flowers and ferns glowing in a starry sky of midnight blue. The full-sized quilt, made in Maine, was pictured in Cyril Nelson's *Quilt Engagement Calendar* for 1983, plate 49.

American quilters rarely interpreted traditional appliqué designs in wool, and just as rarely used a dark shade for the background with light appliqué motifs. The quilt suggests a mysterious mood, inviting a story about whispers in a garden at midnight. A contact between a female spy and her lover perhaps?

Real life spy stories were not so romantic and deal with prosaic things such as pincushions and egg shells. It's quite difficult to know the truth about Civil War spies. Many stories are well embellished and a few seem to be no more than the myths we call urban legends today. In 1862, Southerner Ada Bacot recorded in her diary that she'd heard from a friend about a friend who'd "just returned from Richmond where a young lady had received a few days since, from a young friend of hers now living in Washington City, a present of a simple pincushion. It struck her as being so simple a present to risk so much to send it, that she suspected it might be for some purpose, so she ripped it, and found a letter written on fine French paper [about McClellan's plans to attack Virginia]. The letter was sent immediately to the War Office." A friend of a friend of a friend? A story so far removed from the teller is probably just a story.

Carte de visite photograph. Unknown woman, about 1865, Connecticut.

Another Richmond woman, Elizabeth Van Lew, spied for the Union and her tale is well documented. Like many wealthy Southern girls, she was educated in Philadelphia. There she fell under the influence of an abolitionist, who convinced her of slavery's evils. "Bet" never married and she freed her family slaves before the War. Once War arrived, she refused to keep her Union feelings quiet and became an outcast in the Confederate capitol. She spent her family fortune on supplies for the Union prisoners she visited and thumbed her nose at the city by serving extra abundant dinners to fellow Union sympathizers on Confederate fast days.

Playing the role of pariah to the fullest, she eventually adopted the persona of "Crazy Bet" Van Lew, a spinster in her mid-forties who muttered and sang to herself as she walked through the city. She conveyed information about Richmond's defenses to General Ulysses Grant by secreting coded notes in her servants' shoes and inside hollowed eggs she had delivered to Army kitchens.

Bet received letters with disappearing ink from General Benjamin Butler. A note from "Uncle Thomas" that discussed the new babies in the family was transformed by an acid bath and heat to a series of questions from Butler. "Will there be an attack in North Carolina? How many troops are there?" Another letter concerning illness in Uncle Thomas's neighborhood read when decoded, "Please name a place and set a time you will meet me. You must be sure and name a place that will not endanger my own personal liberty." Bet's duty was to get Butler's letter to its intended recipient.

After the War Bet was rewarded with a position as Richmond's post master during Reconstruction days, but the job didn't last long. The letters of her later years are often disjointed ramblings about conspiracies against her. Crazy Bet, still shunned by Richmond society, began to slip into her wartime role.

A Yankee Spy in Richmond: The Civil War Diary of "Crazy Bet" Van Lew, edited by David D. Ryan. (Stackpole Books, Mechanicsburg, Pennsylvania, 1996) (pg. 83)

Diary entry, April 23, 1862. *A Confederate Nurse: The Diary of Ada W. Bacot,* edited by Jean V. Berlin. (University of South Carolina Press, 1994) Pg. 109.

How to Make the *Midnight Garden* Quilt
40" x 50"
Pattern drawing on center foldout

FABRIC REQUIREMENTS
- **Background fabric:** 1-5/8 yards of blue plaid
- **Basket:** 11" square of a stripe or ticking
- **Stars:** 2/3 yard of assorted light stripes. To make the model quilt, we used three colorways of the same light stripe — 1/2 yard of a light blue-and-cream stripe to make 32 stars, 6" x 30" to make 5 red-, black-and-cream striped stars, and 6" x 24" to make 4 red-, black-and-tan striped stars. We used the same darker stripe to bind the quilt.
- **Stems & leaves:** 3 fat quarters
- **Flowers:** 3" x 8" rectangle of red
  5" x 30", or a fat eighth, of off-white
  6" x 9" of a light stripe
  7" square of butternut
  3" x 7" rectangle of medium gold
- **Binding:** 1/2 yard

PREPARING THE BACKGROUND FABRIC
Wait until you've finished the appliqué to trim the background fabric to size. Mark horizontal, vertical, and diagonal placement lines by folding the quilt and pressing in each direction. After the appliqué is complete, trim to 40-1/2" x 50-1/2".

APPLIQUÉ
Use your favorite method to appliqué the shapes. We used the technique described in our book *Quiltmaker's Guide to Fine Machine Appliqué.* We've given you an overview on page 30 of this book.

Refer to the placement lines on the pattern drawing to arrange the basket of flowers on the background fabric. After you've completed that appliqué, refer to the quilt photo to add the stars or scatter them as you wish. The stars on our inspiration quilt were placed very randomly.

Western Sun

The inspiration for this quilt by Karla Menaugh was a photo of an antique quilt published by the 1980s quilt shop in San Rafael, California, called Mary Strickler's Quilt. Owners Linda Reuther and Julie Silber always called the quilt the Living Room quilt, and we have no name for the combination design of a framed star in a set of flying geese. When we hang the quilt, the geese fly north and west, so the name Western Sun seemed a good one.

We usually think of the Underground Railroad as a path navigated by the North Star. Escaping slaves set their sights north to Ohio, New York, Boston and Canada, but in the west the Underground Railroad sometimes went west.

We see mere glimpses of the lives of people in slavery. Only occasionally did someone write down their memories. One who did was Henry Clay Bruce, a young man who lived as a slave in Missouri until March 30, 1864. Although Lincoln's Emancipation Proclamation had been in effect for over a year by that date, nothing had changed for Bruce and his African-American neighbors in central Missouri. He was courting a young woman belonging to a man named Farmer, who banned him from the property. A slave like Bruce, who could read the newspapers and tell the others they were entitled to freedom, was a danger. The couple were forbidden to see each other.

In his autobiography, Henry Clay Bruce didn't mention Miss Farmer's first name, but he told the story of how they decided to escape to the free state of Kansas west of the Missouri River. They met at 9 o'clock on a night in March. She had "her worldly effects tied up in a handkerchief and I took her up on the horse behind me. . . .We avoided the main road and reached Laclede in safety, where we took the train for St. Joe, thence to Weston, where we crossed the Missouri River on a ferry boat to Fort Leavenworth, Kansas."

Like many others escaping slavery they traveled at night, pursued by their irate owners. Because Henry knew the local roads well he didn't need to navigate by the North Star, as so many other runaways did. Luckily, the slave owners never caught up with them. Henry had a gun and was prepared to fight to the death. "How could I have done otherwise in the presence of the girl I loved, one who had forsaken mother, sister and brothers, and had placed herself entirely under my care and protection. . . .I was braver that night than I have ever been since."

Once across the Missouri the runaways were free. They married and raised four children, living in Leavenworth and Atchison, Kansas, in the years after the war. Henry and his wife moved to Washington D.C. where he became a manager in the U.S. Pension Office. Henry's younger brother Blanche K. Bruce, who also followed the western sun out of slavery to Kansas, served a term (1875-1881) as a Senator from the state of Mississippi, our first African-American senator.

H.C. Bruce, *The New Man: 29 Years a Slave, 29 Years a Free Man* (New York, Negro Universities Press, 1969)

Midnight Garden

Blind Man's Fancy

How to Make the *Western Sun* Quilt
45-1/4" x 45-1/4"

FABRIC REQUIREMENTS
- **Medium butternut:** 2-1/4 yards of plaid & prints
- **Dark butternut or light brown:** 1 yard of assorted plaid & prints
- **Off-white:** 1-1/2 yards of assorted fabrics
- **Note:** We used an easy square/rectangle method to construct the flying geese and the points of the Western Sun block. This method takes more fabric, but you can make 332 extra sawteeth, approximately 1-3/4" unfinished, at the same time as you make the blocks for this quilt. We trimmed some of those sawteeth to 1-1/2" unfinished and used them to make the **Little Blue Baskets** quilt on page 20. For this method, you will need 2-1/2 yards of medium butternut and 2 yards of assorted off-whites.
- **Binding:** 5/8 yard

WESTERN SUN BLOCKS
You will need to make
- five full Western Sun blocks, 9" finished
- four half-blocks
- four quarter blocks.

There are three ways to make the star.

Traditional method — You can piece the entire block, or appliqué part of it.
- Using templates B1, C, and D1, you can piece the star points onto the center circle, A.
- Or, you can use templates B2, C and D1 to piece an eight-pointed star and then appliqué template A, the circle, on top.
- You also will need template D2 for half-blocks and the quarter blocks. Refer to the piecing guides.

Easy Sew method — We liked this method because we didn't have to deal with any inset or curved seams. It takes more fabric, but is fast and easy to sew and also results in 64 additional small sawtooth squares to use for another project.

For each Sun, make a sawtooth star block with the points off-centered so that the center circle can be appliquéd on top. Cut
- five 4-1/4" squares, white, for the block centers
- one 6-1/2" square, white, cut diagonally from corner to corner in both directions to make the center of the half-blocks
- two 3-1/2" squares, white, cut diagonally from corner to corner in one direction to make the center of the quarter-blocks

Traditional pieced Western Sun block

B1
D1
C
A

Piece 8-pointed star, then appliqué circle

B2
D1
C

Piece off-center sawtooth star, then appliqué circle

D1
4-1/4" square

Easy-sew off-center flying geese unit

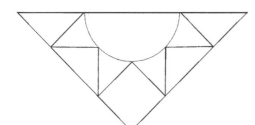

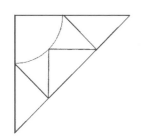

- 64 3-1/8" squares, white for the Sun points
- 32 3-1/8" x 4-1/4" rectangles, butternut
- 24 3-1/8" squares, butternut, for the block corners

To make the Sun points, draw diagonal lines across each of the 3-1/8" off-white squares and then sew two of those squares to each 3-1/8" x 4-1/4" rectangle as explained on page 12 in "Marking and Sewing the Flying Geese, Heirloom and a Spare Method." The center point on each set will be approximately 2-1/8" from the cut edge of the block.

Assemble the Sun blocks as shown, then appliqué a circle (or partial circle) to the top of each, matching the edges of the circle to the inner points.

MAKING THE FRAMES FOR THE WESTERN SUN BLOCKS

Each block, even the half- and quarter-square blocks, are framed by two narrow borders with cornerstones. At the edges of the half- and quarter-square Western Sun blocks, you will need to replace the cornerstones with triangles.

First, cut

- 32 medium/dark rectangles, 1-1/4" x 9-1/2", for the first border
- 24 light butternut squares, 1-1/4" for the first cornerstones
- 4 light butternut squares, 2-5/16", cut in half diagonally from corner to corner to yield 16 triangles to replace the edge cornerstones on the first border
- 32 medium/dark rectangles, 2-1/4" x 11", for the second border
- 24 light butternut squares, 2-1/4" for the second border cornerstones
- 4 light butternut squares, 3-3/4", cut in half diagonally from corner to corner to yield 16 triangles to replace the edge cornerstones on the second border

To sew the frames onto the full blocks,

- add 1-1/4" x 9-1/2" rectangles to two opposite sides of each block
- sew 1-1/4" cornerstones to each end of ten 1-1/4" x 9-1/2" rectangles, and sew these units onto the other sides of the blocks.
- repeat the above steps with the 2-1/4" x 11" rectangles and the 2-1/4" cornerstones.

To sew the frames onto the half-square blocks,

- sew a small triangle onto one end of four 1-1/4" x 9-1/2" rectangles, and sew these units onto one side of the half-blocks.
- sew a 1-1/4" cornerstone to one end and a small triangle onto other end of four 1-1/4 x 9-1/4" rectangles, and sew these units onto the other side of the half-blocks.
- repeat the steps with the larger triangles and the second border rectangles and cornerstones.

To sew the frames onto the quarter-square blocks,

- sew a triangle onto each end of the remaining border rectangles, and add one set to each quarter-square block.

FLYING GEESE

You will need to make 124 flying geese, plus four extra partial sets for the edges of the quilt. To make the geese, use the traditional method or an easy "heirloom & a spare" method that provides 252 extra 1-3/4" unfinished sawteeth to use in another project.

Traditional method — Use your rotary cutter to cut one large off-white triangle and two small butternut triangles for each flying geese block:

- Large off-white triangle. Cut 5-1/4" squares, then cut diagonally from corner to corner in each direction to yield four triangles each. You will need to cut 32 squares to yield the 128 triangles needed for this quilt.

- Small butternut triangles. Cut 2-7/8" squares, then cut in half diagonally from corner to corner in one direction to yield two triangles each. You will need to cut 126 squares to yield the 252 triangles needed for this quilt.

- Small extra butternut triangles for partial units at edge of quilt. Cut one 4-1/8" square and cut in half diagonally from corner to corner in both directions to yield four triangles.

Sew two butternut triangles to the short sides of a large off-white triangle to make each flying geese unit. Make 124 flying geese. Use the extra pieces to make the partial units, explained below.

Heirloom & a spare method — Use simple squares and rectangles to assemble the geese as shown on page 12, doing a little extra sewing as you go to yield 252 additional smaller sawteeth:

- From the off-white fabric, cut 128 rectangles, 2-1/2" x 4-1/2".
- From the butternut fabric, cut 252 squares, 2-1/2".
- Also from the butternut fabric, cut one 4-1/8" square and cut in half diagonally from corner to corner in both directions to yield four triangles. You will use these small extra triangles in partial units at the edge of quilt.

- Follow the directions on page 12 to make 124 flying geese. Use the extra pieces to make the partial units.

Putting together sets of flying geese —

When your flying geese are complete
- sew together 16 sets of 7 flying geese and four sets of two flying geese

- Using the extra flying geese and additional triangles (or squares!), make two of each of the following sets to be used at the quilt's edges. Trim the excess as shown after you've sewn the blocks onto the quilt.

Top edge　　**Right edge**
Add an extra triangle to the bottom right or left side of a flying geese block

Left edge　　**Bottom edge**
Sew butternut triangles onto one end of the white "geese," & assemble in pairs.

+

MARKING AND SEWING THE FLYING GEESE, HEIRLOOM AND A SPARE METHOD

- Draw a pencil line diagonally corner to corner on the back of each square. Draw a second pencil line 1/2" away from the first line.

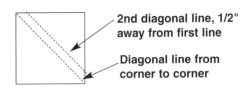

2nd diagonal line, 1/2" away from first line

Diagonal line from corner to corner

- Place a square on top of a rectangle, right sides together, lining up the edges at one end as shown. (fig. A)

- Stitch on both diagonal lines.

- Cut between the diagonal lines. The stitched triangle that you have cut off is a "Spare Square." (fig. B) Press it open, and you will see that it is a sawtooth square. Set this square aside for another project.

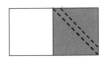   

Fig. A   **Fig. B**

- Now, go back to the rectangle, which looks like it's missing a corner but still has a triangle sewn across one end. Press the triangle up so it completes the rectangle corner. (Fig. C)

Fig. C   **Fig. D**

- Place another square on top of the other end of the rectangle, right sides together, lining up the edges as shown. (Fig. D)

- Stitch on both diagonal lines.

- Cut between the diagonal lines to remove another Spare Square. Set this square aside for another project.(Fig. E)

- Go back to the rectangle and press the second triangle up to complete the corner. (Fig. F)

Fig. E   **Fig. F**

SEWING THE QUILT TOGETHER

- Arrange the blocks as shown in the photo, placing the five full Western Sun blocks in the center of the quilt and adding the half-square blocks at the center edges and the quarter-square blocks at the corners.

- Place the strips of 7 flying geese between all the blocks, then add the sets of two geese at the intersections between blocks. Add the partial blocks at the edges of the quilt.

- Sew together in diagonal rows.

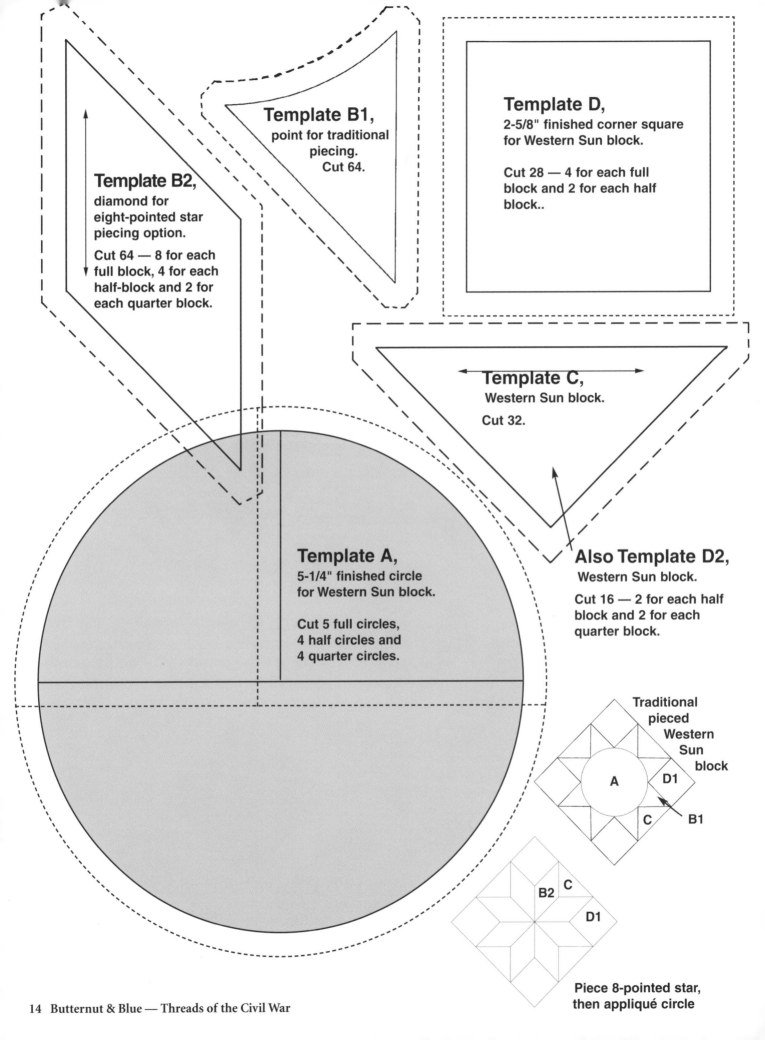

Template B1,
point for traditional piecing.
Cut 64.

Template B2,
diamond for eight-pointed star piecing option.

Cut 64 — 8 for each full block, 4 for each half-block and 2 for each quarter block.

Template D,
2-5/8" finished corner square for Western Sun block.

Cut 28 — 4 for each full block and 2 for each half block..

Template C,
Western Sun block.

Cut 32.

Template A,
5-1/4" finished circle for Western Sun block.

Cut 5 full circles, 4 half circles and 4 quarter circles.

Also Template D2,
Western Sun block.

Cut 16 — 2 for each half block and 2 for each quarter block.

Traditional pieced Western Sun block

A

D1

C

B1

B2

C

D1

Piece 8-pointed star, then appliqué circle

Basket in the Briars

Karla Menaugh's inspiration was a two-color, two-block quilt made after the Civil War. She remade it in butternuts and blues to recall the stories of the women who aided the Butternuts and Bushwhackers, the irregular guerrillas who fought behind Union lines.

Missouri, a Union state during the Civil War, had long been home to Southern sympathizers. During the winter of 1860-1861 after Lincoln's election, many state officials, including the governor, wanted to join the Confederacy, but the Union Army's powerful presence insured that Missouri remained in the Union. With such divided loyalties, the state evolved into a small, yet miserable version of Hell, home to more skirmishes than any place but Virginia.

In the initial months of the War, twenty-two year old John McCorkle from Savannah, Missouri, joined the regular Confederate Army attempting to gain control of the state. When the regulars retreated, McCorkle deserted rather than travel South. His intention to live peacefully at home was interrupted when the Federals attempted to impress him into the State Militia by threatening his cousin Mollie Wigginton with imprisonment if he refused to join. Women were not often jailed in the rest of the country, but conditions in Missouri quickly deteriorated to the point where revenge, recrimination and murder of civilians, both men and women, became too common.

McCorkle joined William Quantrill's band of guerrilla fighters, justifying in an autobiography his own acts of terror by citing affronts to the women in his family and neighborhood. "Mrs. Carter, a widow seventy years of age – compelled – at the hour of 12 o'clock at night to ride fourteen miles horseback, facing a bitter snowstorm, to the town of Independence, where she was lodged in jail for feeding rebel soldiers, her two boys being in the Confederate Army." The Federal Army knew the bushwhackers survived only through aid from their sisters, mothers and sweethearts who carried baskets full of food to their camps in the bushes, washed their laundry and sewed their clothing, lavishing extra time and needlework talent on the fancy embroidered "guerrilla shirts" worn under butternut jackets.

MORE ➤

Basket in the Briars, continued

McCorkle's sister Charity McCorkle Kerr and sister-in-law Nannie Harris McCorkle were arrested in 1863 in Kansas City as they traded a wagon load of wheat for flour. A neighbor identified the young women as rebel sympathizers, likely to use the flour to bake bread for McCorkle and his fellow butternuts. The McCorkle women were taken to a makeshift Federal prison with seven other young women accused of feeding and harboring bushwhackers. The stone building was so unstable that it collapsed on the prisoners, killing Charity and three others. Like other Southern sympathizers, John McCorkle believed the disaster to be no accident. "Imagine, if you can, my feelings, a loved sister foully murdered and the widow of a dead brother seriously hurt by a set of men to whom the name assassins, murderers and cutthroats would be a compliment. This foul murder was the direct cause of the famous raid on Lawrence, Kansas. We could stand no more – .We were determined to have revenge."

The escalation of retaliation between Confederate butternuts and soldiers in Union blue continued after Charity Kerr's death. The quilt recalls her and all the women who set out after dusk every evening, carrying baskets of food into the woods of the border states from Northern Virginia, through Southern Indiana and Northern Kentucky to Western Missouri.

Three Years with Quantrill, A True Story Told by His Scout John McCorkle, by O.S. Barton, (Armstrong, Missouri: 1914). Reprint: Norman: University of Oklahoma Press, 1992. Pp. 120-3.

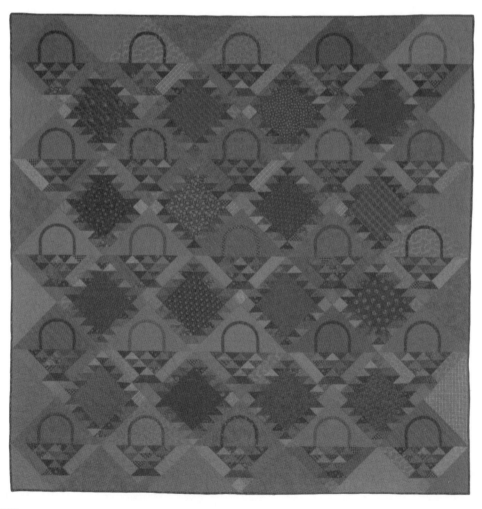

Butternut & Blue

Our Flag

We adapted the design from a flag crocheted in the early twentieth century, possibly designed to hang in a window during World War I or II. Many Civil War veterans wrote their reminiscences during those years. Those who had lived in border states often recalled the role of the flag in declaring whose star was in ascendance.

How to Make the Our Flag Filet Crochet Wallhanging

APPROXIMATELY 15" x 17"

PATTERN DRAWING AT LEFT

YOU WILL NEED
- **Crochet cotton no. 30, ecru, about 1400 yards**
- **Steel crochet hook, U.S. size 11**

To filet crochet the block,
Beginning at the bottom edge, ch 259.

ROW 1: Dc in 4th ch from hook and in next 3 sts. *Ch 2 sk 2 sts, dc in next st and in next 3 sts. Repeat from * across ending with a 4 dc solid mesh <sm>. 43 sm across. Ch 5, turn.

ROW 2: *Dc in 4th st of first sm, 2 dc over ch-2, 1 dc in next dc, ch 2, Repeat from * across ending with an open mesh <om>.

ROWS 3-85: Work following the diagram. Fasten off.

Abbreviations:
ch - chain
dc - double crochet
sk - skip
st(s) - stitch(es)
sm - solid mesh
om - open mesh

To frame, cover an 18" x 22" piece of foam-core with dark fabric, blue or red. Pin the crocheted block to the fabric and place in a frame.

Butternut & Blue
Midnight
Garden

Half of block. Reverse for other half.
Make a 15" bias strip, 3/8" finished, for the
center stem. Make about 100" of 1/4" finished
bias strips for the other stems.
See other directions, page 7.

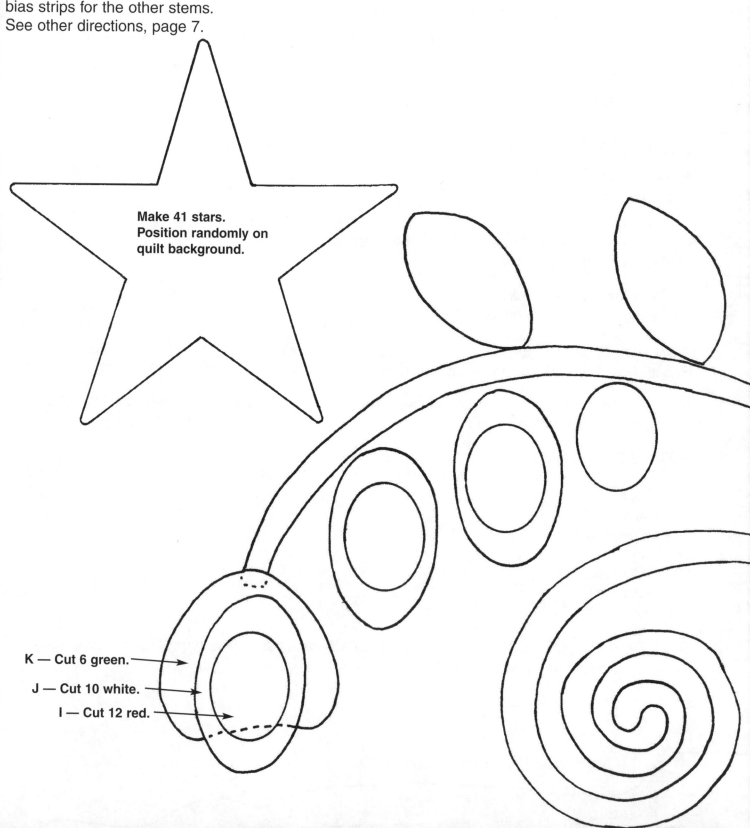

Make 41 stars.
Position randomly on
quilt background.

K — Cut 6 green.

J — Cut 10 white.

I — Cut 12 red.

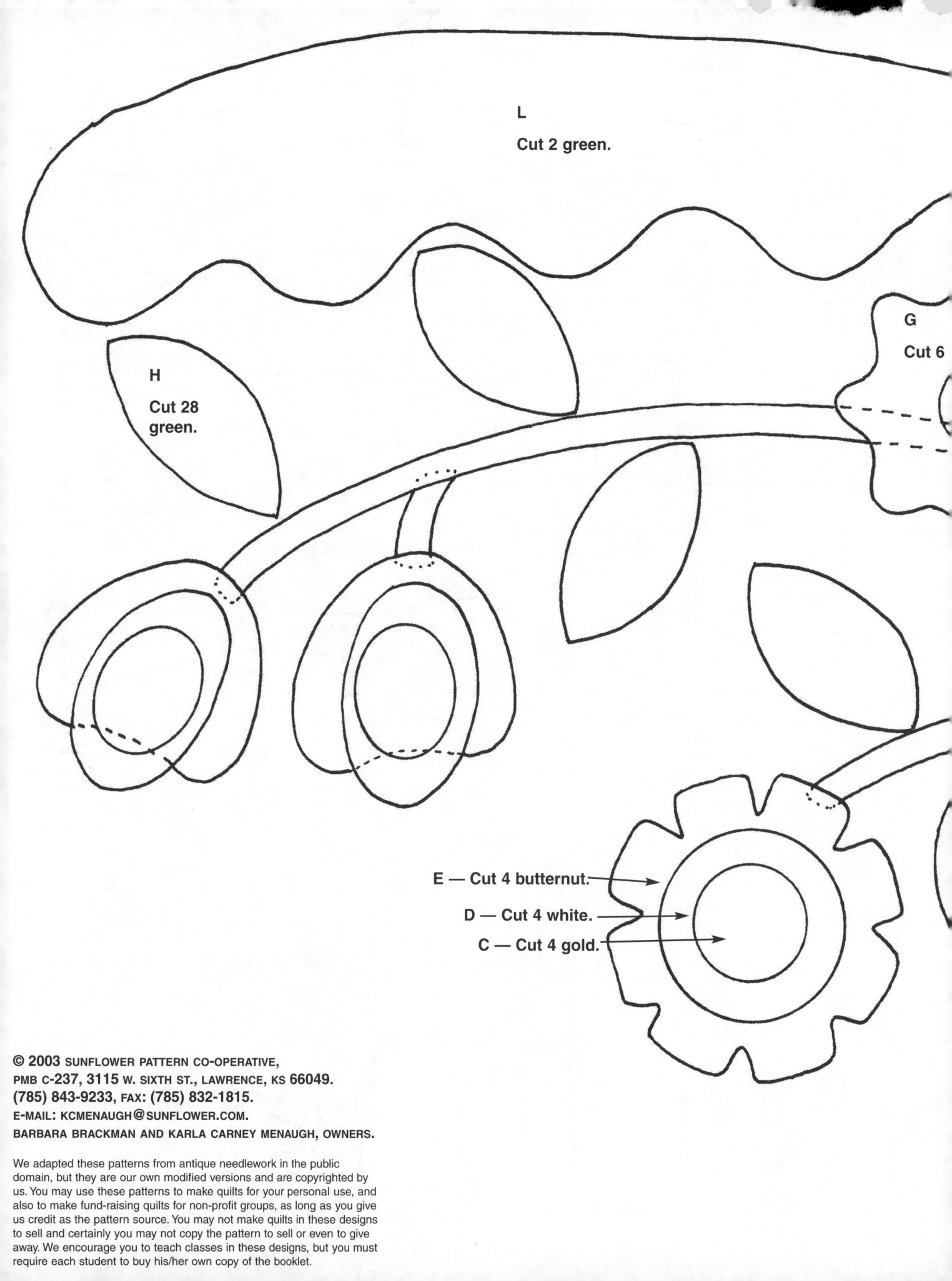

L

Cut 2 green.

G

Cut 6

H

Cut 28 green.

E — Cut 4 butternut.

D — Cut 4 white.

C — Cut 4 gold.

How to Make the *Basket in the Briars* Quilt
85" x 85"

FABRIC REQUIREMENTS
- **Note:** We used a wide variety of butternuts and blues to make this quilt. To replicate the look, buy assorted fat quarters and other cuts as indicated below. But a two-fabric quilt also would be stunning, as was our inspiration quilt, a red-and-white version made in 1900. If you wish to use only two fabrics, you would have less fabric waste. Buy 3-1/2 yards of blue and 5 yards of butternut.
- **Butternut:** 5/8 yard of four different prints, plus 13 assorted fat quarters.
- **Blue:** 17 fat quarters
- **Binding**: 5/8 yard

You will need to make
- 25 basket blocks, 12" finished
- 16 sawtooth square blocks, 12" finished
- 16 setting triangles
- 4 corner triangles

CUTTING INSTRUCTIONS
From the blue, cut
- 25 basket handles
- 25 squares, 4-1/8", cut diagonally from corner to corner in both directions to yield four triangles each. These triangles will form the top edge of each basket.
- 16 squares, 8-1/2"
- Use the rest of the fabric to make the sawteeth.

From the butternut, cut
- 4 squares, 18-1/4", cut diagonally from corner to corner in both directions to yeld four triangles each. These triangles are the setting triangles for the edges of the quilt.
- 2 squares, 9-3/8", cut diagonally from corner to corner in one direction to yield two triangles each. These are the corner triangles for the quilt.
- 13 squares, 12-7/8", cut diagonally from corner to corner in one direction to yield two triangles each. These are the backgrounds for the basket handles. You will need only 25. You can cut the remaining triangle into squares for sawteeth.
- 50 rectangles, 2-1/2" x 8-7/8", for the sides of the baskets. You will need to make a 45-degree diagonal cut at one end of each. Half will point in one direction, the other half in the opposite direction.
- 57 squares, 2-1/2". 25 of these are for the baskets, 32 for the sawtooth squares.
- Use the rest of the fabric to make the sawteeth.

Sawteeth — You will need to make 488 sawteeth that finish to 2", 2-1/2" unfinished. That's a lot of sawteeth, but you'd be amazed at how fast it is to make them once you get going. See page 31 for general instructions on making sawteeth.

Sawtooth Squares — Make 16.

- Sew together 32 sets of four sawteeth as pictured below. Sew them onto opposite sides of each 8-1/2" square.

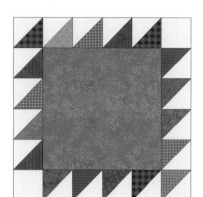

- Sew together 32 sets of five sawteeth and one 2-1/2" square as shown below. Sew these onto the top and bottom of each 8-1/2" square.

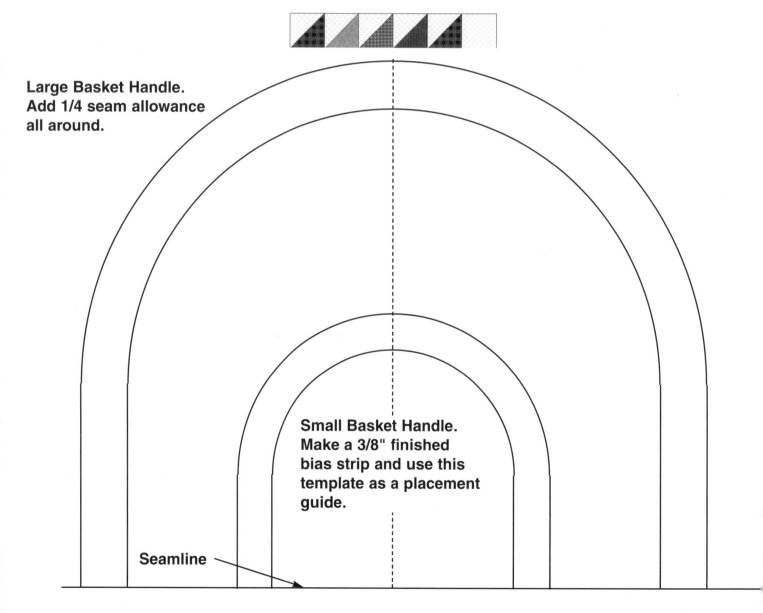

**Large Basket Handle.
Add 1/4 seam allowance
all around.**

**Small Basket Handle.
Make a 3/8" finished
bias strip and use this
template as a placement
guide.**

Seamline

Baskets — Make 25.

- Sew together 25 sets each of sawteeth and triangles as pictured below.

1 triangle & 3 sawteeth   1 triangle & 2 sawteeth   1 triangle & 1 sawtooth

- To make the body of the basket, sew together one of each of the above sets, plus one more triangle.

- To make the sides of the basket, use the 2-1/2" butternut squares, 2-1/2" x 8-7/8" rectangles with angles cut at one end, and the remaining sawteeth to make 25 each of the sets pictured below. Sew the sides onto the basket bodies.

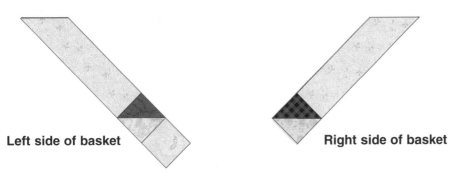

Left side of basket   **Right side of basket**

- Appliqué the handles to the 12-7/8" triangles. Sew a basket top to each basket bottom to complete the basket blocks.

- Arrange the baskets and sawtooth squares as pictured, with five rows of baskets across and five rows down. Place the sawtooth squares between the baskets. Put the setting triangles and corners at the edges of the quilt. Sew together in diagonal rows.

Little Blue Basket

T he name has two meaning. The pattern literally is a little blue basket. The Little Blue is a river in western Missouri that formed valleys and caves along the Kansas/Missouri border. The landscape along the Little Blue provided hiding places and refuge for the Butternuts during the Civil War.

How to Make the *Little Blue Basket* Quilt
19" x 19"

FABRIC REQUIREMENTS
- **Note:** We used 170 of the leftover sawteeth from the Western Sun project to make this little quilt. If you need to make your own sawteeth, add 1/3 yard each of butternut and off-white assorted fabrics.
- **Off-white:** assorted fabrics equal to a fat-quarter
- **Blue:** 1/2 yard, including binding

You will need to make
- 5 basket blocks, 6" finished
- 4 sawtooth setting triangles
- 4 sawtooth corner triangles
- sawtooth border, 1" finished

CUTTING INSTRUCTIONS
From the blue, cut
- 5 bias strips, 3/4" x 7-3/4", for the basket handles. Use a bias tape maker to fold them to 3/8" finished strips.
- 1 square, 6-7/8", cut diagonally from corner to corner in both directions to yield four triangles each. These are the setting triangles for the quilt.
- 2 squares, 3-3/4" each, cut diagonally from corner to corner to yield two triangles each. These are the quilt corners.

From the off-white, cut
- 3 squares, 6-7/8", cut diagonally from corner to corner in one direction to yield two triangles each. These will be the backgrounds for the basket handles. You will need only five. You can cut the sixth one into pieces for the rest of the quilt.
- 10 rectangles, 1-1/2" x 4-7/8", for the sides of the baskets. You will need to make a 45-degree diagonal cut at one end of each. Half will point in one direction, the other half in the opposite direction.
- 13 squares, 1-1/2"

Sawteeth

- We used 170 of the "extra" sawteeth we made when we used the "Heirloom and a Spare" method of assembling the Western Sun quilt. If you used the same method, trim the sawteeth to 1-1/2" for this quilt.

  If you need to make new sawteeth, see page 31 for instructions. You will need an additional 1/3 yard each of butternut and off-white.

Baskets

- The little baskets are sewn together in the same way as the large baskets, described on page 19.
- We cut the big basket handles from a template, but because this handle is so thin, you can make it from a 3/8" bias strip. Use a 3/8" bias tape maker to fold the 3/4" bias strips into 3/8" finished strips. Use the placement guide on page 18 to position the strip on the handle backgrounds and appliqué into place.

Sawtooth setting triangles and corners

- Make two of each of the following sets to be used at the quilt's edges. Because the blocks are set together diagonally, you will need to trim a sawtooth or a square at the end of each strip to make it even with the edge of the large triangle.

Carte de visite photograph of the Sanders family, Oshkosh, Wisconsin, about 1865.

Side edges
Sew a sawtooth to both ends, then trim even with the triangle

Top & bottom edges
Sew a square to both ends, then trim even with the triangle

Bottom left, top right corners
Sew a sawtooth to one end and a square to the other, then trim even with the corner triangle

Top left, bottom right corner
Sew a sawtooth to one end and a square to the other, then trim even with the corner triangle

Assembly and Border

- Arrange the blocks, referring to the photo and directions. Sew together in diagonal rows.
- Sew together four sets of 17 sawteeth each, all facing the same direction. Sew two of the sets to the sides of the quilt.
- Sew a sawtooth to each end of the remaining sets, reversing the direction of the sawtooth at one end as shown in the photo. Sew these two sets onto the top and bottom the quilt.

Sawtooth Table Runner

Of course, the women on the Civil War didn't use table runners like this. But we like them, and this one is made from a block that is very similar to the Sawtooth Square we used in *Basket in the Briars.*

How to Make the *Sawtooth Table Runner*
17" x 54"

FABRIC REQUIREMENTS
- **Butternut:** 3 fat quarters
- **Blue:** 3 fat quarters. Buy four to have enough to make the binding.

You will need to make
- 3 sawtooth square blocks, blue, 12" finished
- 4 sawtooth setting triangles, butternut

CUTTING AND SEWING INSTRUCTIONS
- Cut 3 blue squares and 2 butternut squares, 8-7/8." Cut each diagonally from corner to corner in one direction to yield two triangles.

- Mix the blue triangles and sew together to make 3 squares.

- Cut two 4-1/8" butternut squares and cut diagonally from corner to corner in both directions to yield eight triangles. Use these for the edges of the setting triangle strips.

- Use the rest of the fabric to make 96 sawteeth, finishing to 2" each. See page 31 for directions.

- Sew the sawteeth onto the squares and large triangles as shown below. Sew the small triangles you have cut from the 4-1/8" butternut squares onto the sawtooth setting triangles.

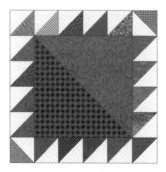 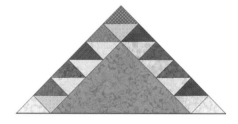

- Arrange the blocks and sew together in diagonal rows.

Blind Man's Fancy

We picked the pattern not for the name, but for its appearance and its resemblance to several Union and Union Star designs. This particular block has only one recorded name, Blind Man's Fancy, from the Ladies Art Company's patchwork catalog of the late nineteenth-century. The name is a little puzzling, if not tasteless, but the Ladies Art Company advertised that they offered patterns with the most bizarre and grotesque names.

Blind Man's Fancy does call to mind, however, the terrible numbers of wounded veterans who survived the war to live the rest of their lives without sight or with missing limbs. One of the most amazing American quilts, pictured in Sandi Fox's book, *Wrapped in Glory: Figurative Quilts and Bedcovers*, depicts a soldier going off to the Civil War and returning blinded. In one block, a guide dog on a leash leads him. A typed commentary left by the maker, possibly Emma Sivey Stahl, or her daughter, notes: "Angels are guarding the blind man and his dog. Notice how he is groping his way."

Carte de visite photograph, unknown woman, about 1865.

Diaries, letters and memoirs often tell of disabled veterans. Captain Charles Searle who described the sweetheart flag found in prison on page 27, was hit in the head in a battle and left for dead with a permanent injury to his spine.

After the War the G.A.R. (Grand Army of the Republic) veteran's organization did much to aid the disabled men and their families. The women's auxiliary, known as the Women's Relief Corps, raised money for veterans with needlework sold at ladies' fairs and other festivities.

An undated newspaper clipping, probably from the 1880s, tells the story of Carrie Manning, the wife of an invalid veteran, who donated a beaded flag to her local Women's Relief Corps meeting room. Carrie, who was herself blind, made a flag of "red, white and blue ribbon. – The stars are of beaded work and the black walnut flagstaff is trimmed with a vine of exquisite workmanship terminating in a fullblown water lily, all beaded work." Carrie's work was truly a blind woman's fancy. A poem accompanied her donation:

> "Sisters, accept the gift I bring,
> It is a grateful offering;
> These little stars that shine so bright
> Were formed without the gift of sight.
> These stripes that on the flag you see
> Were measured, too, and cut by me;
> I fain my gratitude would show,
> And you'll excuse defects, I know..."

Sandi Fox, *Wrapped in Glory: Figurative Quilts and Bedcovers, 1700-1900.* (Los Angeles: Los Angeles County Museum of Art, 1990) Pg. 111.

How to Make the *Blind Man's Fancy* Quilt

56" x 56" — 9 BLOCKS, 16" FINISHED

FABRIC REQUIREMENTS

- Part of the charm of this quilt is the wide variety of fabric. We are part of a nine-person sewing group, and each person made one of these blocks for Barbara. You may wish to talk some of your friends into making blocks for each other, too, or at least trading squares of fabric.
- **Large-scale print:** 9 fat eighths for the center stars. If you have bigger pieces of some of the prints, use some to make the sawteeth around the outer edge of the blocks.
- **Medium butternuts and browns:** 2 yards of assorted fabrics. For each block you will need to cut two 6-7/8" squares to yield the four triangles around the inner star, so buy 8 or 9 quarter yards and use the remaining fabric for the sawteeth.
- **Off-white:** 2 yards of assorted fabrics. A variety of fat eights and fat quarters would work.
- **Border:** 3/4 yard
- **Binding:** 5/8 yard

CUTTING AND SEWING INSTRUCTIONS

To make the center star-in-a-square block, for each block cut

- 1 square of large floral, 4-3/4" for the center
- 4 squares of large floral, 3", cut diagonally from corner to corner in one direction to yield two triangles each. These triangles will be the star points.
- 1 square of light fabric, 5-1/2", cut diagonally from corner to corner in both directions to yield four triangles. These will be the background behind the points.
- 4 squares of light fabric, 2-5/8", for the block corners
- 2 squares of medium butternut, 6-7/8", cut diagonally from corner to corner in one direction to yield two triangles each. These will form the square around the star block.

To make each block,

- sew the small dark triangles onto the two equal sides of the large triangles to make four flying geese units.
- Sew two of the flying geese units onto opposite sides of the center square.

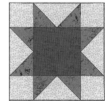

- Sew the light squares onto each end of the other two flying geese units, then sew these units onto the other sides of the center square to complete the star.
- Sew the medium butternut triangles onto the sides of the star block to form the star-in-a-square block.

Our Flag antique crocheted picture
and appliquéd wall quilt

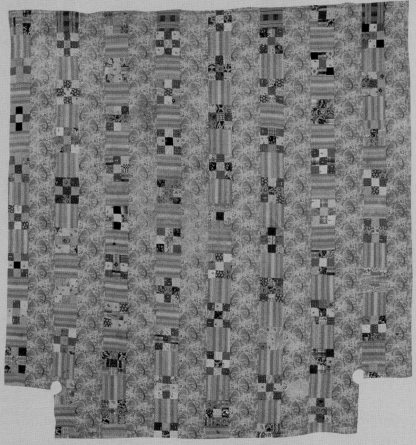

Road to Richmond,
antique at top right and
reproduction at bottom
right

*Sawtooth Square Table
Runner,* **above**

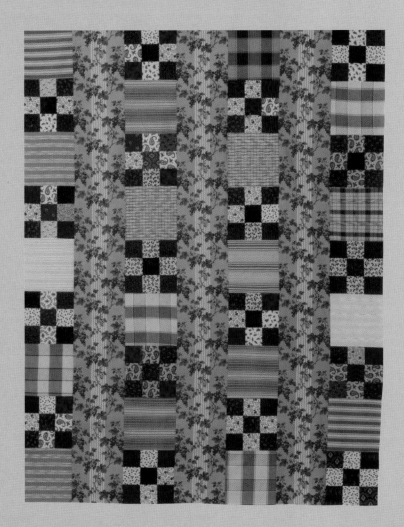

To make the sawteeth border for each block

- Cut 4 squares from light fabric, 2-1/2" for the block corners
- Make 24 sawteeth, 2" finished, for each block; 216 total. See page 31 for general directions on how to make sawteeth.
- Sew the sawteeth together in sets of 6, with the points facing away from the center as shown. Sew the 2-1/2" light squares onto the ends of two of the sawteeth sets for each block.
- Sew a set of six sawteeth onto two opposite sides of each block.
- Finish each block by sewing a set of six sawteeth and two squares onto the other sides of the block.

SETTING AND BORDER

- Arrange the blocks in rows of three and sew together.
- For the border, cut five strips 4-1/2" x the width of the fabric. Sew these together to make two strips that are 4-1/2" x 48-1/2" and two strips that are 4-1/2" x 56-1/2".
- Sew the short strips onto the sides of the quilt. Add the longer strips to the top and bottom to finish the quilt top.

SETTING OPTION

Another great way to set this quilt is to put 4-1/2" sashing strips between the blocks. To make this option

- Buy 3/4 yards of fabric for the sashing and cut it into five strips 4-1/2" x the width of the fabric. From the strips cut six strips 4-1/2" x 16-1/2" and sew these between the blocks in the horizontal rows.
- Sew the rest of the strips together to make two 4-1/2" x 48-1/2" strips and sew them between the horizontal rows.
- For the border, buy one yard of fabric. Cut six strips 4-1/2" x the width of the fabric. Sew these together to make two strips that are 4-1/2" x 56-1/2" and two strips that are 4-1/2" x 64-1/2".
- Sew the short strips onto the sides of the quilt. Add the longer strips to the top and bottom to finish the quilt top.

Road to Richmond

O ur small quilt is a close copy of an antique nine-patch that looks to be from the 1850s, the years when sectionalism between North and South slowly pushed the country along the road to Civil War. The original quilt, with its cut-out corners, was designed for a four-poster bed. The fabrics, especially the printed plaids that separate the nine-patches, and the strip setting mark it as a pre-Civil War quilt. The backing, which is pictured on the back cover, is quite unusual. It looks to be home-dyed with butternut. One does not often see home-dyed backings on cotton quilts, and butternut is a dye that rarely was used with cotton quilt fabric.

Karla Menaugh re-created a small version of the strippy nine-patch, which we've called Road to Richmond. Richmond was the capital of the Confederacy, and the ultimate goal of the Yankee forces throughout the Civil War. Once Richmond was captured in 1865, the Confederacy was doomed. But the Road to Richmond actually began much earlier, with the political posturings and broken promises of the first half of the nineteenth century.

How to Make the *Road to Richmond* Quilt
54" x 66"

FABRIC REQUIREMENTS

- **Large-scale print for setting strips:** 2 yards.
- **Medium/dark prints:** Assorted small cuts totaling 3/4 yard.
- **Light prints:** Assorted small cuts totaling 2/3 yard.
  Plaids: Small cuts totaling 1-1/4 yards.
- **Binding**: 5/8 yard

CUTTING AND SEWING INSTRUCTIONS

Make 28 nine-patch blocks, 6" finished

- Cut 252 squares, 2-1/2". Make 135 medium/dark and 117 light.
- Sew the squares together in rows of three to make 28 nine-patch blocks. Make five blocks with light squares on the corners; make the rest with the dark squares on the corners.

To put the quilt together

- Cut 27 plaid squares, 6-1/2".
- Cut four strips of large-print fabric, 6-1/2" x 66-1/2" each.
- Sew 5 rows of alternating nine-patches and plaid squares as pictured.
- Sew the strips together, alternating pieced strips with the long fabric strips.

Our Flag

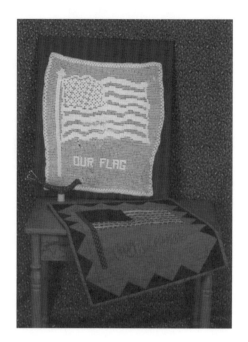

We adapted the design from a flag crocheted in the early twentieth century, possibly designed to hang in a window during World War I or II. Many Civil War veterans wrote their reminiscences during those years. Those who had lived in border states often recalled the role of the flag in declaring whose star was in ascendence.

In Tennessee, rebels and unionists lived side by side, as Northern and Southern armies vied for power. Martha Turner Searle remembered living in Memphis during the summer of 1864 while her husband served as part of an occupying Iowa regiment. She occasionally attended church services where "the members were strongly Rebel in sentiment – . No one would sit near a Yankee Captain's wife and they gave me plenty of room to pass out, fearing apparently that if they touched but the hem of my garment they would be defiled."

The Confederate women announced their loyalties in subtle ways. Martha remembered that some preferred to "walk in the middle of the street, rather than to pass under the Stars and Stripes, which hung in front of the barracks. When my husband finally draped flags quite across the street, it was amusing to watch the disdainful air with which they surveyed them as they approached and the contempt with which they would turn and go blocks out of their way, rather than to submit to the humiliation of allowing its folds to wave above them."

During that summer, Martha's husband Captain Charles Searle was taken prisoner, his second capture. Years later, he recalled how important the Union flag was to the prisoners in Augusta, Georgia. As the Fourth of July approached they decided to flaunt their patriotism with a homemade flag. "A committee was appointed to canvass among the denizens of the prison, thinking to find one who had a red shirt, another with a blue one and one with a possible white one, who would be willing to sacrifice a part of the garment for the occasion. Imagine the surprise to find a comrade who had picked up a small flag on the Shiloh battlefield, and wrapped it over his heart under his outer garments and carried it all these months concealed from view! When it was brought forth – imagine the cheering and joy – I cannot describe it." Fortunately for Searle and his fellow prisoners the Confederate guards were "indulgent and seemed to enjoy it themselves."

The small flag was probably a handmade "Sweetheart Flag" stitched for a Union soldier who'd lost it when he died at Shiloh. His grieving wife or sister would never know that her flag survived to cheer prisoners far away from his grave.

"Civil War Reminiscences," edited by Helen H. Cresap, *Annals of Iowa,* Volume 42, Number 1, Summer, 1973. Pp. 75-76.

For instructions on making the crocheted picture and the appliquéd wallhanging, see the foldout sheet in the center of this book.

Flag Sewing Kit

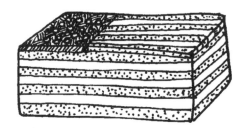

Our inspiration was a little silk and wool sewing box, which very well may have been a patriotic Union knicknack. The image of the flag was not apparent at first glance. The blue wool has bled into the red and white striped silk, making it two shades of purple rather than a patriotic stripe. And the blue field is just a rectangle until white pins representing stars are placed in the proper constellation.

The original kit still has its inventory of sewing tools, a thimble, a tape measure and two spools of thread, one in a tiny bag made from a delaine dress fabric. A wooden spool, now empty, is stitched inside the bag. The seamstress guided her thread through a small hole in the bag, which prevented the spool from rolling away.

Many women made such patriotic sewing tools during the Civil War. Needlebooks, pincushions and thread holders were sold at Ladies' Fairs to fund the hospital work of the Sanitary Commission. Sweethearts and daughters sent sewing kits for soldier's packs. "Comfort Bags" contained needle and thread, pins and a scissors with a few peppermints.

FABRIC AND FINDINGS
- **Red striped fabric:** about 10" x 14"
- **Blue fabric:** about 2" x 4-1/2"
- **Cardboard or template plastic:** about 8" x 10"
- **Findings:** a pinch of wool roving or other stuffing for the pin-cushion, 13 white glass-headed pins. Optional: a thimble, tiny scissors, spool of thread & needlebook to store inside the box.

CUTTING AND SEWING INSTRUCTIONS
From the cardboard or plastic, cut
- 3 sides: 4 1/2" x 1-1/2"
- 3 ends: 1-1/2" square
- 1 lid: 3-1/4" x 1-1/2"

From the red stripe (be sure the stripes are going the long way so the box looks like a flag), cut
- 3 sides 5" x 4"
- 3 ends 4" x 2"
- I lid 4" x 3-3/4"

From the blue fabric, cut
- 1 field 1-3/4" x 4"

PREPARE THE SIDES

You'll need to make finished sides of the box which are then whipped together by hand. You can do this in one of two ways:

- Make a little pillow case for all the striped pieces, by folding each piece of fabric in half with the right sides together. Stitch along two sides and turn inside out. Insert the cardboard and whip stitch the last side closed.

- Or, you can wrap each piece of cardboard like a little present and whip the seams closed. The seams will go on the inside of the box where they won't be seen.

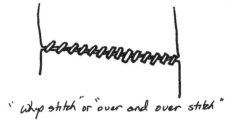

" whip stitch" or "over and over stitch"

You'll need three sides, three ends and a lid.

CONSTRUCT THE BOX

- Attach the three sides together as shown, stitching on the inside of the seams so the stitching barely shows on the outside of the box.

- Add one of the end pieces which holds the pincushion by whipstitching it to the base of the box 1-1/2" in from the left side.

- Adjust that end to stand up as you turn up the sides of the box.

- Add the ends of the box by whip stitching them on three sides.

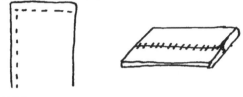

- Stuff the pincushion part under the field with wool roving or other stuffing.

- Fold the blue field fabric in half and whip stitch it to the box above the stuffing.

- Add the lid to the box by whip stitching it to the right end.

FINISH THE KIT

- Stick pins in an arrangement, a circle, star or square field.

- Add sewing tools to the box.

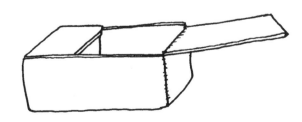

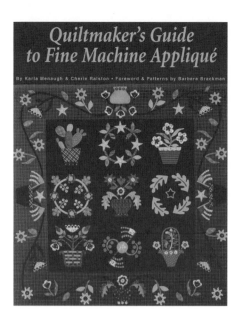

Machine Appliqué

We used a freezer-paper machine-appliqué technique that looks a lot like hand appliqué. Our book, *Quiltmaker's Guide to Fine Machine Appliqué,* offers step-by-step lessons in the technique and is a great reference for anyone who wants to machine-stitch quilts that look hand appliquéd.

If you'd rather hand appliqué your projects, read Elly Sienkiewicz's *Twelve Ways to Appliqué.* It's another great reference guide.

To use our machine-appliqué technique

- Trace the pattern pieces, without seams, onto the shiny side of freezer paper.

- Cut them out and iron shiny side down to the wrong side of the fabric. Cut out, adding 3/16" seam allowance.

- Run a glue stick along the edge of the freezer-paper and fold the fabric over the paper, leaving raw edges only where a piece will be under another.

- Start with an oversized background. Position the appliqué pieces on the background and pin well. Or, better yet, baste with Roxanne's Glu-Baste-It, a thin, white glue that comes in a plastic bottle with an applicator tip. Dot glue around the folded-under edges of your appliqué, and finger press them into place on the background fabric. This will eliminate the bumps and ridges caused by the pins, and you won't prick your fingers while you're sewing, either.

- Use thin, all-cotton thread that matches your appliqué pieces. We used DMC 50 machine embroidery thread. Metler 60-weight, 2 ply cotton thread, or Aurifil 50-weight cotton thread are other good choices.

- The machine stitch that looks the most like hand appliqué is the Variable Overlock. On most machines, it takes three straight stitches forward, then one zig-zag stitch followed by three more straight stitches and another zig-zag, etc. To make this stitch mimic hand appliqué, override the default settings to make it much narrower and shorter. For the best setting on your machine, compare a stitched sample to the full-size samples shown at left. Sew right on the edge of the appliqué, with the straight stitches going "in the ditch" into the background fabric and the zig-zag stitches catching the edge of the appliqué shape.

- Once everything is stitched down, soak or wash the entire piece in cold water and toss it in the dryer with a dry towel. When it is dry, trim the underneath fabric within 1/4" of the appliqué stitches. Take out the freezer paper. Press from the wrong side and trim to to the correct size.

Our Vari-Overlock stitch, adjusted for very short, very narrow stitches. The straight stitches go into the background fabric, "in the ditch" beside the appliqué. The zig-zag stitches catch the top of the appliqué shape. If your machine doesn't have this stitch, try making your zig-zag stitch short and narrow.

Making Sawteeth

There's an easy-to-remember formula for making sawteeth —

- Add 7/8" to the finished size of the sawtooth square, and cut one light and one dark square in that size.

- Draw a diagonal line from corner to corner on the back side of each of the light squares.

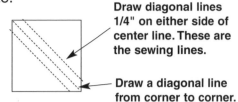

Draw diagonal lines 1/4" on either side of center line. These are the sewing lines.

Draw a diagonal line from corner to corner.

- Draw a line 1/4" on each side of the diagonal line. Sew on those lines.

- Cut the squares apart on the center line. For each pair of squares, you will have two sawteeth. Iron the seam toward the dark fabric.

If you're unsure of your sewing or cutting, you can start with squares that are 1" bigger than the finished size of the block. Make the sawteeth, then use your rotary ruler and cutter to trim them to the correct size.

To make a large quantity of sawteeth, you can draw a grid of squares on the back of the light fabric. Draw diagonal lines through the corners of the grid, and sew 1/4" on either side of the lines. Cut the grid into squares, and cut the squares in half on their center lines. You'll have two sawteeth for every grid square.

Since most of the quilts in this book are scrappy, we cut most of our fabric into small grids — two squares across and two squares down. For the 2" sawteeth, we started with 6" squares, drew an "X" from corner to corner on the back of the light square, and sewed 1/4" on both sides of the center lines. We cut the square in half in both directions, then cut along the diagonal center lines to make 8 sawteeth at a time. We trimmed those to 2-1/2" squares for perfect sawteeth. If we had smaller pieces of fabric to use, we cut them into 3" squares.

Credits

**Sunflower, woodcut by
Barbara Brackman, 2003**

Authors:
 Barbara Brackman
  & Karla Menaugh
Photography:
 Jon Blumb

Published by
Sunflower Pattern Co-operative
5103 McGregor Drive
LaGrange, KY 40031

Our thanks go to Lori Kukuk, who machine quilted most of the projects in this book, and to Shirlene Wedd, who sewed the binding on most. Also to Pam Mayfield, who machine quilted both **Our Flag** quilts and **Little Blue Basket**, and to Rosie Mayhew, who quilted **Western Sun.** We are very fortunate to have such great quilters in our area. They just keep getting better every day!

Our thanks also goes to Cherie Ralston, who recreated the filet crochet pattern for **Our Flag.** Cherie is truly a woman of many talents!

We thank Christine Kraft, who designed our new logo for us.

And, thanks to our Thursday sewing group, who provide so much inspiration and encouragement and who made the **Blind Man's Fancy** blocks for Barbara as part of a block exchange. The blocks were made by Alma Allen, Barbara Brackman, Shauna Christensen, Pam Mayfield, Karla Menaugh, Cherie Ralston, Deb Rowden, Jean Stanclift, and Terry Thompson.

Karla Menaugh made the quilt tops for this book, with the exception of blocks in **Blind Man's Fancy.** Barbara Brackman made the new **Flag Sewing Kit.**

SUNFLOWER PATTERN CO-OPERATIVE

Barbara Brackman and Karla Menaugh founded the Sunflower Pattern Co-operative in 1999 to produce quilt patterns inspired by historically significant quilts and other needlework. Our plan was to encourage other quilt artists to design projects as well. We have been proud to have published quilt designs by Shauna Christensen, Kathleen Glasco, Pam Mayfield, Cherie Ralston, Jean Stanclift, and Shirley and Shirlene Wedd.

In 2002, Barbara, Karla, and Cherie Ralston collaborated on two books, the *Quiltmaker's Guide to Fine Machine Appliqué* and *Fat Quarter Fancywork.*

The Sunflower line of quilt patterns includes special series on quilts from the Civil War and classic crib quilts. All the patterns offer history notes written by Barbara, quilt historian and author of *Quilts from the Civil War* and *Civil War Women, Creating Your Family Quilt, Prairie Flower: A Year on the Plains,* and *Clues in the Calico,* as well as the *Encyclopedia of Pieced Quilt Patterns* and *Encyclopedia of Appliqué.* Another series, *Patchwork Pals,* is intended to offer beginning patterns that adults and children can produce together.

To see other publications from Sunflower Pattern Co-operative, ask at your local quilting store, check our website at quiltsunflower.com or write to us at the address at left.